A Note From Rick Renner

I am on a personal quest to see a "revival of the Bible" so people can establish their lives on a firm foundation that will stand strong and endure the test as end-time storm winds begin to intensify.

In order to experience a revival of the Bible in your personal life, it is important to take time each day to read, receive, and apply its truths to your life. James tells us that if we will continue in the perfect law of liberty — refusing to be forgetful hearers, but determined to be doers — we will be blessed in our ways. As you watch or listen to the programs in this series and work through this corresponding study guide, I trust you will search the Scriptures and allow the Holy Spirit to help you hear something new from God's Word that applies specifically to your life. I encourage you to be a doer of the Word He reveals to you. Whatever the cost, I assure you — it will be worth it.

> Thy words were found, and I did eat them;
> and thy word was unto me the joy and rejoicing of mine heart:
> for I am called by thy name, O Lord God of hosts.
> —Jeremiah 15:16

Your brother and friend in Jesus Christ,

Rick Renner

Supernatural Weight Loss

Copyright © 2023 by Rick Renner
1814 W. Tacoma St.
Broken Arrow, OK 74012-1406

Published by Rick Renner Ministries
www.renner.org

ISBN 13: 978-1-6675-0362-2

eBook ISBN 13: 978-1-6675-0363-9

How To Use This Study Guide

This five-lesson study guide corresponds to *"Supernatural Weight Loss" With Rick Renner* **(Renner TV)**. Each lesson in this study guide covers a topic that is addressed during the program series, with questions and references supplied to draw you deeper into your own private study of the Scriptures on this subject.

To derive the most benefit from this study guide, consider the following:

First, watch or listen to the program prior to working through the corresponding lesson in this guide. (Programs can also be viewed at **renner.org** by clicking on the Media/Archive links or on our Renner Ministries YouTube channel.)

Second, take the time to look up the scriptures included in each lesson. Prayerfully consider their application to your own life.

Third, use a journal or notebook to make note of your answers to each lesson's Study Questions and Practical Application challenges.

Fourth, invest specific time in prayer and in the Word of God to consult with the Holy Spirit. Write down the scriptures or insights He reveals to you.

Finally, take action! Whatever the Lord tells you to do according to His Word, do it.

For added insights on this subject, it is recommended that you obtain Rick Renner's book *My Peace-Filled Day*. You may also select from Rick's other available resources by placing your order at **renner.org** or by calling 1-800-742-5593.

TOPIC

Supernatural Weight Loss

SCRIPTURES

1. **1 Peter 5:7** — Casting all your care upon him; for he careth for you.

GREEK WORDS

1. "casting" — ἐπιρρίπτω (*epirripto*): to hurl, throw, or cast; to throw or fling something with great force; in secular literature, it often pictured the flinging of a garment, bag, or excess weight off the shoulders of a traveler and onto the back of a beast, such as a donkey, camel, or horse

2. "all" — πᾶσαν (*pasan*): all; all-inclusive; absolutely everything

3. "care" — μέριμνα (*merimna*): anxiety; used to describe affliction, difficulty, hardship, misfortune, trouble, or a complicated circumstance that arises as a result of problems that develop in life: problems that are financial, marital, job-related, family-related, business-oriented, or anything else that concerns us in the earthly realm

4. "upon" — ἐπί (*epi*): on; upon; literally, onto

5. "for" — ὅτι (*hoti*): precisely because

6. "he careth" — μέλει (*melei*): aware, concerned, interested, or thoughtful; one who notices and gives meticulous attention; depicts a thorough and careful focus on the needs of another

7. "for" — περί (*peri*): around; concerning; everything concerning you

SYNOPSIS

The five lessons in this study on **Supernatural Weight Loss** will focus on the following topics:

- Supernatural Weight Loss
- 'A Bible Verse I Did Not Like'
- How To Stop Worrying
- Steps To Move From Anxiety and Worry to a Peace-Filled Life
- How To Let Peace Umpire Your Emotions

The emphasis of this lesson:

First Peter 5:7 gives us the key to supernatural weight loss. Instead of worrying or carrying the burden of our own anxieties, we need to cast our cares on the Lord. As Rick Renner shares his personal testimony with worry, we see a clear example of how vital casting our care on the Lord is to our lives. It is time for you to shed the excess weight of the cares you've been carrying and finally be set free!

In First Peter 5:7, the apostle Peter wrote:

> **Casting all your care upon him; for he careth for you.**

In this program, Rick shares that this verse really helped him become free of worry in his life. As a young man, he struggled with worry and found it creeping into almost every area of his life. But when Rick finally understood what it meant to cast his cares on the Lord, this verse liberated him and helped him throw off all kinds of excess weight that God never intended for him to carry.

In the following section, Rick shares about the worry he experienced in his early years of life, marriage, and ministry.

Rick's Early Years With Worry

When I was younger, I worried all the time. In fact, I actually thought if I was not worried about something I was being irresponsible.

I remember hearing certain language in our church like, "Do you have a burden for souls?" And although it's good to be concerned about peoples' salvation, as a young man this kind of language led me to understand that if I was serious about my spiritual life I was supposed to be burdened about something all the time.

I began to live life carrying around burdens about all kinds of things. And if I had a day where I was burden free or carefree, I began to feel guilty as if somehow I was missing the mark. I would think, *Rick, you've got to get serious. You need to be burdened by something. You need to be carrying some kind of spiritual weight.*

I felt like I needed to be burdened all the time. When Denise and I got married, I carried this thinking into our marriage. And when we started our first ministry, serving in a large Baptist church, our pastor continually talked about having a burden for this and having a burden for that, which, again, confirmed to me that I always needed to be burdened about something.

I was literally spinning with worry, and it was consuming my life. I worried about whether or not I was really saved. Denise and I both questioned our salvation, so we worried about it all the time. I worried about people who were unsaved, and I worried about whether I was ministering successfully or well enough — I just worried all the time.

My friends told me, "Rick, you need to stop this worrying," but I worried so much I ended up in the hospital with bleeding ulcers. I even had to get a blood transfusion because I was so weak and had lost so much blood.

At the hospital, the doctor came in and sat on the side of the bed. He said, "Rick Renner, you are too young to be eaten up with worry and care. This is not right. You've got to learn how to throw this off." And I said, "Well, doctor, I don't know how to do that. I'm just concerned and worried all the time." But he told me again, "You've got to put an end to this. This will kill you. This will end your life early."

When the doctor got up and left my room, it just so happened that the TV was on. Now, remember, blood was still flowing into my arm from the transfusion. And as I sat there watching the news, they announced that a new killer disease had been found. It was AIDS, but they didn't even have a name for it yet. The news reporters said that people were concerned the disease had even infiltrated blood banks in hospitals across the United States.

Well, there I was lying in the bed looking at this blood flowing into my arm, and I began to think, *Wonderful. Maybe I have just been infected with this new disease.* I began to worry that I had been infected with this silent killer. In fact, even after I left the hospital I worried and worried about it.

Finally, one day Denise said, "Rick you need to go to the doctor and take a test so you can get set free from this worrying." So I went to the doctor. I walked in and very quietly said, "I'm here to take an AIDS test." After several weeks, I went back in to get the results, and when I went in, the reception area was full. A nurse who knew me from church saw me and said, "Brother Rick, it's so good! We want to tell you that you were absolutely clear. You don't need to worry about AIDS." She said it so loud that I knew people in the room heard it. And when I walked out of the room, I began to worry about what all those people must be thinking who heard I'd been in for an AIDS test.

I continued to worry about everything. I worried and worried about our finances. I worried whether we would have enough food to feed our family. I worried whether our house was going to be sufficient. I worried about what we had, what we didn't have, and what was going to happen in the future. I worried about people's opinions of me — I literally lived under a ton of worry.

But in one moment I was set free, and I literally threw off the burdens I had been carrying.

Casting All Your Care Upon the Lord

Rick carried the weight of his worry completely on his own. He worried about everything and didn't know how to stop. But the truth is, the Lord never intended for any of us to live under the burden of worry and stress. First Peter 5:7 tells us, "*Casting* all your care upon him; for he careth for you."

The word "casting" is the Greek word *epirripto*, and it means *to hurl*, *to throw*, or *to fling something with great force*. This is not describing an action done lightly; it is a motion done with great force, as in someone throwing something off of himself.

In the secular world, it often pictured the flinging of a garment or a bag or throwing excess weight off the shoulders of a traveler and onto the back of a beast of burden, like a donkey, camel, or horse.

If someone was traveling, and the weight that he was carrying was too much for him to carry, he would ask somebody to bring him a beast of burden. Once the donkey, camel, or horse came alongside him, the traveler would then shove upward and push that burden off of his back and onto the back of the beast. The burden didn't disappear; it was just transferred from the traveler's shoulders onto the back of the beast of burden.

In this verse, we literally have an invitation from Jesus. He says, "Let me be your beast of burden. I'll walk right alongside you. Your burden won't disappear, but I'll carry it for you. It's too much for your shoulders."

The burden of stress, anxiety, fret, or worry is too much for us. When we try to carry it on our own, it breaks us. It affects our health, our peace, and our relationships — it affects everything. But Jesus is saying, "Let me walk alongside you. Push up, shove, and roll over all your burdens onto me. I'll carry them for you. Your burdens won't disappear, but the weight of them will be transferred to me so you can walk freely and enjoy your life." That's what this verse is saying.

Peter also said we are to cast *all* our care upon Jesus. The word "all," the Greek word *pasan*, literally means *all*. It is an all-inclusive term that means *absolutely everything*.

There are some people who will talk to everyone *except* God about their worries. And when someone asks them, "Have you talked to the Lord about this?" They respond, "Oh, I don't want to bother the Lord with my worries." But, honestly, the Lord is the *only* one who can help them. He is right there alongside us, and He wants us to cast all of what we're worried about onto His shoulders — absolutely everything.

The word "care" is the Greek word *merimna*, and it appears not only in this verse but in many of the verses we'll look at in future lessons of this teaching. It denotes *anxiety* and is used to describe *affliction or hard times, difficulty, hardships, misfortune, trouble,* or *complicated circumstances that arise as a result of problems that have developed in someone's life.*

So think about any troubles or circumstances you are facing that are complicated. That's what this word "care" describes. It depicts problems that are financial, marital, job-related, family-related, business-oriented, or anything else that concerns you in this earthly realm. That means everything that concerns you is included in this word "care."

And this verse tells us to cast all of our care *upon* Jesus. The word "upon" is the Greek word *epi*, which literally means *on, upon,* or literally *onto*. Again, it is the picture of Jesus coming alongside us like a beast of burden, saying, "Your shoulders are not designed to carry this. It's going to affect your emotions, your marriage, and your relationships. It's going to break your health. This is just too much for you to carry, so please, shove your burdens onto my back and I will carry it for you."

Jesus Cares for You

First Peter 5:7 goes on to say, "Casting all your care upon him; *for* he careth for you."

The word "for" in Greek is the word *hoti*, and it means *precisely because*. With this word, Peter was getting very specific. He was speaking of how intentionally and thoughtfully Jesus cares for us. The word "careth" is the Greek word *melei*, and it means *to be aware; to be concerned; to be interested;* and *to be thoughtful.*

Jesus is aware of our situation, He is concerned about our situation, He is interested in our situation, and He is thoughtful about our situation. The word "careth" depicts *one who notices or who gives meticulous attention* and pictures *a thorough and careful focus on the needs of others,* which means Jesus is not ignorant or blind to the fact that we're carrying a load we should not be carrying. He knows all about it.

If your needs are financial, marital, job-related, family-related, business-oriented, or anything else that concerns you in this earthly realm, Jesus knows about it, and He is aware, concerned, interested, and thoughtful about it. He is meticulously giving attention to it and has a very careful focus on your needs.

This verse goes on to say Jesus cares *for* you. The word "for" is the Greek word *peri*, and the word *peri* always describes *a perimeter*. It's where we get the word "perimeter," which denotes a circumference or something that surrounds you. A better translation would be: "He cares about everything around you and everything concerning you."

Rick's Supernatural Weight Loss

When Rick realized the true meaning of First Peter 5:7, it transformed his life. He was liberated from the weight and constant burden that worry had created in his life. Here Rick shares the end of his personal testimony about how the Lord truly set him free:

> There I was, worrying and worrying about everything, and then one day I walked into our church auditorium. It was vacant because it was not a day when a service was taking place. And in that auditorium, I said to the Lord, "I can't live like this.

This worry is just eating me alive." I went down to my knees and said, "Lord, right now today I'm throwing everything on you including my care and concern about whether I'm saved or not."

Looking back, it seems ridiculous to have said that. I was as saved as I could be, but I was genuinely worried that I just *thought* I was saved but wasn't *really* saved.

But that day, after living under a ton of weight and worry, I got on my knees in front of the altar and said, "Okay, Jesus, this is it. I'm not going to live like this anymore. If I'm not saved, there's nothing else I can do to be saved. I've asked you not once but probably ten thousand times to save me, and I'm tired of asking. Either I'm saved or I'm not, but this is the end of it."

"I have also worried about what people think of me, and Lord, my worry doesn't change anything about what people think about me. The truth is people are probably not even thinking about me. I'm done with this. I'm done with worry."

And when I got up off my knees, it was like a ton of weight had been lifted off me. To get to that place, I had to come to the end of myself where I was finally willing to surrender all my worry and care and roll it over onto Jesus.

After that powerful moment on my knees before the Lord, I didn't worry for a long, long time. Later in life, I did have one more episode with worry — and I'm going to tell you about that in these lessons — but after that last bout with worry, I really have walked free of worry in my life. I really have!

Jesus Wants To Set You Free!

There is no reason for you to worry. Jesus never intended for the cares of this life to rest upon your shoulders. Instead, First Peter 5:7 shows us that we really can roll our burden over onto the Lord and walk freely without the weight we've been carrying. Rick's personal testimony is a powerful example of that.

Today Jesus is calling out to you. He's saying, "I'm right here. Let me carry this for you. Cast your burdens over onto me." You don't have to walk in stress, anxiety, or worry anymore. You can choose to walk freely alongside Jesus and let Him carry all the weight for you.

In the next lesson, we'll take a closer look at a verse in the New Testament that Rick did not like at first but eventually learned to love.

STUDY QUESTIONS

**Study to shew thyself approved unto God, a workman that needeth
not to be ashamed, rightly dividing the word of truth.
—2 Timothy 2:15**

1. What does First Peter 5:7 tell us to do? How is this different from Rick's attitude in his early years of life and ministry?
2. What areas of Rick's life did worry affect? Was there ever a time when worry had a positive influence on him?
3. First Peter 5:7 says that Jesus "careth" for you. The word "careth" is the Greek word *melei*. What does this word mean, and why is it important in the context of this verse?
4. Read Philippians 4:6 and 7. How does knowing the meaning of First Peter 5:7 influence your understanding of this passage?

PRACTICAL APPLICATION

**But be ye doers of the word, and not hearers only,
deceiving your own selves.
—James 1:22**

1. Rick shared that at a young age he heard phrases like, "Do you have a burden for the lost?" in his church. Did you also have a similar experience? Can you think of any other examples where worry might have been misunderstood as a necessary or positive part of life while you were growing up?
2. Think about a time in your life when things felt out of control and you tried to carry the weight and burden of your circumstances on your own. Take a moment to journal about how you handled that situation then and how you would handle it now armed with First Peter 5:7.
3. What is one area of your life where you need to cast your cares on Jesus? Pray and ask the Lord to come alongside you in this situation and then throw the weight you've been carrying onto His back.

TOPIC

'A Bible Verse I Did Not Like'

SCRIPTURES

1. **1 Peter 5:7** — Casting all your care upon him; for he careth for you.
2. **Matthew 6:25** — Therefore I say unto you, Take no thought for your life, what ye shall eat, or what ye shall drink; nor yet for your body, what ye shall put on. Is not the life more than meat, and the body than raiment?
3. **Matthew 6:26** — Behold the fowls of the air: for they sow not, neither do they reap, nor gather into barns; yet your heavenly Father feedeth them. Are ye not much better than they?
4. **Matthew 6:27** — Which of you by taking thought can add one cubit unto his stature?
5. **Matthew 6:28** — And why take ye thought for raiment? Consider the lilies of the field, how they grow; they toil not, neither do they spin.
6. **Matthew 6:29** — And yet I say unto you, That even Solomon in all his glory was not arrayed like one of these.
7. **Matthew 6:30** — Wherefore, if God so clothe the grass of the field, which to day is, and tomorrow is cast into the oven, shall he not much more clothe you, O ye of little faith?
8. **Matthew 6:31** — Therefore take no thought, saying, What shall we eat? or, What shall we drink? or, Wherewithal shall we be clothed?
9. **Matthew 6:32** — (For after all these things do the Gentiles seek:) for your heavenly Father knoweth that ye have need of all these things.
10. **Matthew 6:33** — But seek ye first the kingdom of God, and his righteousness; and all these things shall be added unto you.

GREEK WORDS

1. "casting" — ἐπιρρίπτω (*epirripto*): to hurl, throw, or cast; to throw or fling something with great force; in secular literature, it often pictured the flinging of a garment, bag, or excess weight off the shoulders of a traveler and onto the back of a beast, such as a donkey, camel, or horse

2. "all" — **πᾶσαν** (*pasan*): all; all-inclusive; absolutely everything

3. "care" — **μέριμνα** (*merimna*): anxiety; used to describe affliction, difficulty, hardship, misfortune, trouble, or a complicated circumstance that arises as a result of problems that develop in life: problems that are financial, marital, job-related, family-related, business-oriented, or anything else that concerns us in the earthly realm

4. "upon" — **ἐπί** (*epi*): on; upon; literally, onto

5. "for" — **ὅτι** (*hoti*): precisely because

6. "he careth" — **μέλει** (*melei*): aware, concerned, interested, or thoughtful; one who notices and gives meticulous attention; depicts a thorough and careful focus on the needs of another

7. "for" — **περί** (*peri*): around; concerning; everything concerning you

8. "take no thought" — **μὴ μεριμνᾶτε** (*me merimnate*): the particle **μὴ** is a negative with a canceling force; the word **μέριμνα** (*merimna*) depicts anxiety; used to describe affliction, difficulty, hardship, misfortune, trouble, or a complicated circumstance that arises as a result of problems that develop in life: problems that are financial, marital, job-related, family-related, business-oriented, or anything else that concerns us in the earthly realm; as a phrase, it is a prohibition against any type of anxiety or worry about any financial, material, or physical needs

9. "life" — **ψυχῇ** (*psuche*): anything related to life

10. "eat" — **φάγω** (*phago*): food; what one will eat; what is required for life

11. "drink" — **πίνω** (*pino*): drink; required for life

12. "body" — **σῶμα** (*soma*): physical body; physical needs

13. "put on" — **ἐνδύω** (*enduo*): denotes the putting on of clothes

14. "behold" — **ἐμβλέπω** (*emblepo*): to consider; to notice; to observe; to stare; take a thoughtful look at

15. "fowls of the air" — **πετεινὰ τοῦ οὐρανοῦ** (*peteina tou ouranou*): birds of the heavens

16. "for" — **ὅτι** (*hoti*): precisely that

17. "feedeth" — **τρέφω** (*trepho*): not only feeds, but fully nourishes

18. "much" — **μᾶλλον** (*mallon*): comparatively much more

19. "better" — **διαφέρω** (*diaphero*): superior in every way

20. "which" — **τίς** (*tis*): who

21. "taking thought" — **μέριμνα** (*merimna*): depicts anxiety; used to describe affliction, difficulty, hardship, misfortune, trouble, or a complicated circumstance that arises as a result of problems that develop in life: problems that are financial, marital, job-related, family-related, business-oriented, or anything else that concerns us in the earthly realm; being anxious or worrying

22. "add" — **προστίθημι** (*prostithemi*): to add; to increase

23. "one cubit" — **πῆχυς** (*pechus*): a span of about 18 inches

24. "stature" — **ἡλικίαν** (*helikian*): lifespan

25. "take ye thought" — **μέριμνα** (*merimna*): depicts anxiety; used to describe affliction, difficulty, hardship, misfortune, trouble, or a complicated circumstance that arises as a result of problems that develop in life: problems that are financial, marital, job-related, family-related, business-oriented, or anything else that concerns us in the earthly realm

26. "for" — **περί** (*peri*): around; concerning; everything concerning clothes

27. "raiment" — **ἐνδύω** (*enduo*): denotes clothes

28. "consider" — **καταμανθάνω** (*katamanthano*): consider; seriously study

29. "lilies of the field" — **τὰ κρίνα τοῦ ἀγροῦ** (*ta krina tou agrou*): a lily growing wild in the field

30. "grow" — **αὐξάνω** (*auxano*): to grow; to increase

31. "toil" — **κοπιάω** (*kopiao*): labor; the most intense type of labor

32. "spin" — **νήθω** (*netho*): to spin (in worry)

33. "much more" — **πολλῷ μᾶλλον** (*pollo mallon*): much, much more

34. "little faith" — **ὀλιγόπιστος** (*oligopistos*): only occurs five times in the New Testament; little faith; small trust; always used as a rebuke

35. "therefore" — **οὖν** (*oun*): consequently, or as a result of all this

36. "take no thought" — **μὴ μεριμνήσητε** (*me merimnesete*): to be taken as a prohibition; stop worrying; put an end to worrying

37. "saying" — **λέγοντες** (*legontes*): repeatedly saying and saying; here we find that the mouth speaks worry

38. "what" — **Τί** (*Ti*): very specific; this is intense worry; used three times in this verse

39. "wherewithal" — **Τί** (*Ti*): very specific; this is intense worry

40. "Father" — **Πατὴρ** (*Pater*): Father; the One who cares and nourishes

41. "knoweth" — οἶδα (*oida*): knowledge gained by observation, meaning the Father is watching and knows it all

42. "that" — ὅτι (*hoti*): precisely that

43. "need" — χρῄζω (*chredzo*): deficits; needs; necessities

44. "all" — ἅπας (*hapas*): each and every one

45. "but" — δέ (*de*): but instead

46. "first" — πρῶτον (*proton*): first and foremost; as a matter of the first and highest priority

47. "seek" — ζητέω (*zeteo*): to seek very intensively; denotes an intense and thorough searching, not a mere surface investigating; to search for thoroughly and exhaustively

48. "all these things" — ταῦτα πάντα (*tauta panta*): literally, all these things, nothing excluded

49. "added" — προστίθημι (*prostithemi*): added; pictures increase

50. "unto you" — ὑμῖν (*humin*): directly to you

SYNOPSIS

In our first lesson, Rick shared his personal experience with supernatural weight loss. After years of being consumed with worry, Rick discovered how to truly cast his care on the Lord. He was set free from the crippling effects of worry in his life and experienced freedom from that heavy burden for the first time. From Rick's example, we can clearly see that in order to experience supernatural weight loss, we need to cast our burdens onto the Lord.

In this lesson, we will take a closer look at a passage in the Bible that Rick did not like — or understand — for many years. Similar to First Peter 5:7, these scriptures confirm that we need to let go of worry and instead choose to trust the Lord. We were not designed to carry the weight of stress and anxiety in our lives, and in order to experience supernatural weight loss, we need to trust God with *all* of our physical needs.

The emphasis of this lesson:

Don't worry about the physical needs in your life. God already knows what you need to eat, drink, and clothe yourself. Instead of worrying about it, spend your time earnestly seeking His kingdom and His righteousness in your life and trust that He will bring these things to you.

How To Cast Your Care

When we're worried, we become intoxicated with the cares of this life. We don't think right, and we don't see things correctly. We might even say things that we wouldn't normally say. But God did not create us to carry worry, and that is why in First Peter 5:7 the Bible says, "*Casting* all your care upon him; for he careth for you."

As we saw in Lesson 1, the word "casting" is the Greek word *epirripto*, which means *to hurl; to throw; to cast;* or *to throw or fling something with great force*. It describes someone who says, "I'm tired of carrying this weight. It's too much for me," and then hurls it over onto someone else. And in secular literature, the word *epirripto* often depicted the flinging of a garment, bag, or excess weight off the shoulders of a traveler and onto the back of a beast like a donkey, camel, or horse.

Here we have an invitation from Jesus. He is literally saying, "Your shoulders are not made to carry that kind of weight. It will crush you. It will affect your health, and it will affect everything in your life, your marriage, and your relationships." And just like a traveler could call a beast of burden alongside him to take the weight he had been carrying, Jesus says, "Let me come alongside you. I'll walk with you, and you can roll it all over onto me. My shoulders are big enough to carry it all. You can walk freely alongside me, and I'll carry the weight for you."

The verse goes on to say, "Casting *all* your care...." As we saw in the previous lesson, the word "all" is an all-encompassing term, meaning *absolutely everything*. It really means *everything* — whatever is concerning you is included in that word "all."

The word "care" is the Greek word *merimna*, which we will see again later in this lesson. It is the word for *anxiety*, and it was used to describe *affliction, difficulty, hardship, misfortune, trouble,* or *complicated circumstances that arise as a result of problems that develop in life*. This includes problems that are financial, marital, job-related, family-related, business-oriented, or anything else that concerns us in the earthly realm.

If there is anything weighing you down, or if you are dealing with a complicated situation in your life, Jesus has come alongside you, and He is asking you to roll all of your cares onto Him. You were never made to carry that burden on your own. Jesus wants to take that weight for you precisely because He *cares* for you.

The word "cares," or "careth," is the Greek word *melei*, which means *to be aware, concerned, interested, or thoughtful*. It depicts one who notices and gives meticulous attention to someone else. This means that Jesus has His eyes on you, and He knows when you're carrying a weight that you're not designed to carry.

We see clearly in First Peter 5:7 that Jesus wants to come alongside us and carry the burdens we were never meant to carry. And as we choose to throw our cares onto Jesus, we truly will be set free to live without the crippling effect of worry and anxiety in our lives.

Don't Worry About Your Life

Rick shared in the TV program that when he was younger, he did not like the verse Matthew 6:25. Even after studying it in Greek, Rick did not like what it said because it clearly stated to stop worrying. Let's take a closer look at what Matthew 6:25 has to say.

> **Therefore I say unto you, Take no thought for your life, what ye shall eat, or what ye shall drink; nor yet for your body, what ye shall put on. Is not the life more than meat, and the body than raiment?**
>
> **— Matthew 6:25**

The phrase "take no thought" begins with the particle *me*, which means *stop it* and has a canceling force. The next part of the phrase is the Greek word *merimna*, and it is the same word we saw in Lesson 1 for *anxiety*. It describes any kind of *affliction, difficulty, hardship, misfortune, trouble*, or *complicated circumstances in life*.

This includes problems that are financial, marital, job-related, family-related, business-oriented, or anything else that concerns us in the earthly realm. And as a phrase, it is a prohibition against any kind of anxiety or worry that is financial, material, or having to do with the physical realm.

The particle *me* is a very strong prohibition. The Greek literally means *cut it out, stop worrying, put an end to it — right now*.

This verse clearly tells us not to worry about anything at all, which is exactly why Rick disliked it so much. At that time, he did not know *how* to stop worrying. But in this verse, Jesus tells us that it is possible for us to experience supernatural weight loss — we can throw all the weight of our burdens over onto the Lord and not carry them any longer.

And in Matthew 6:25, Jesus specifically tells us not to worry about what we will eat or what we will drink. The word "eat" is the Greek word *phago*, and it describes *what someone eats* or *what is necessary for life*. The word "drink," likewise, describes *what a person drinks* or *what must be consumed in order to live*.

The verse goes on to say, "…Nor yet for your *body*…." The word "body" is the Greek word *soma*, and it refers to *anything having to do with our physical body*, including our health, our physical condition, what we're eating, or what we put on our body. Jesus didn't want us to worry about our physical needs, so much so that He even said, "…Is not the life more than meat [food], and the body more than raiment [clothing]?"

An Environment of Worry

In the program, Rick shares about a time when he watched how his parents dealt with worry. He said:

> When I was a young boy, my family did not have a lot of money. We didn't live on the best side of Tulsa; we kind of lived on "the other side of the tracks."
>
> And we didn't just live on the other side of the tracks — we lived *between* the tracks. Literally, our house was between two sets of railroad tracks, and it was not the finest neighborhood. In fact, it was probably the worst neighborhood in the city of Tulsa.
>
> But that's where we lived, and my sisters and I didn't even know that we were poor. However, I can distinctly remember my parents being really worried. It especially happened every year when it was time for school to begin because it was time to buy clothes for my sisters and me.
>
> I remember my parents having very difficult conversations as my mother would say to my dad, "Ronald, we've got to buy new jeans for Rick, and we've got to buy new clothes for the girls." Or she would say, "Rick needs new shoes," and then I would hear the wrangling and the arguing of my parents going back and forth.
>
> As a child, I felt so guilty that I was growing and needed new clothes because it seemed like such a burden to my parents.

I also remember seeing my dad sitting in front of his little desk in his bedroom on Thursday nights going over the bills. That was always such a tense night in our house. You could nearly cut the air with a knife because of the tension caused by my dad worrying about this bill and that bill, wondering if we would have enough to get by until the next payday.

And that's the environment my sisters and I grew up in, literally worrying about what we were going to eat, what we were going to drink, and what we were going to put on.

Maybe you had a childhood experience similar to Rick's, or maybe you became accustomed to worrying much later in your life. Either way, this is a helpful example of what an environment of worry can do. From a young age, Rick observed his parents responding to the needs of their family with worry, and that made worry a much more natural response for Rick later in his life. But Jesus tells us in Matthew 6:25 that it doesn't have to be this way. He says, "…Is not the life more than meat, and the body than raiment?" And the answer is yes. Yes, it is!

'Behold the Fowls of the Air'

So how do we let go of this stress and worry that wants to rule our lives? Matthew 6:26 tells us, "Behold the fowls of the air: for they sow not, neither do they reap, nor gather into barns; yet your heavenly Father feedeth them. Are ye not much better than they?"

The word "behold" here is the Greek word *emblepo*, which means *consider, notice, observe, stare at*, or *take a thoughtful look at*. Jesus says to really consider and to look closely at the birds around us and watch how they act. They aren't worried about where their next meal will come from, and yet our heavenly Father feeds them.

In the program, Rick recounted a time when he was working on a book in Tel Aviv, Israel. He was sitting on a patio, and he noticed birds everywhere. After people got up from their tables, these birds would land on the table and eat the leftover food. He even saw sparrows eat whole French fries.

Those birds were fat from eating all that food, and Rick remembered thinking this was a great example of what Jesus said in Matthew 6:26. Those birds didn't think about what they were going to eat that day.

Instead, they just showed up at the hotel and had a feast. Their heavenly Father cared for them and fed them. But this verse also says that our heavenly Father cares for us. It says, "Are ye not much better than they?"

The Greek says *comparatively much, much more*, and the word "better" means *superior in every way*. And then in Matthew 6:27, Jesus adds, "Which of you by taking thought can add one cubit unto his stature?"

The *King James Version* says "which," and in Greek, it is the word *tis*, which really means *who*. So in this verse, Jesus is saying, "*Who* of you by taking thought…." And the phrase "taking thought" is, again, the Greek word *merimna*, which describes *anxiety* or *worry*. This means, Jesus really said, "Who of you by being anxious and who of you by fretting and worrying can add one cubic unto his stature?"

The word "add" in Greek is the word *prostithemi*, and it means *to increase* or *to expand*. The measurement "one cubic" describes a span of about 18 inches. And the word "stature" in Greek is the word *helikian*, which means *lifespan*.

So in verse 27, Jesus is telling us, "You can't even add 18 inches to your lifespan by worrying; it is just a waste of your time — a totally futile activity." And then in verse 28, Jesus adds, "And why take ye thought…?"

Again, we see the Greek word *merimna*. Here it also depicts *anxiety*, and it can be used to describe *affliction, difficulty, hardship, misfortune, trouble*, or *complicated circumstances in life*. This includes problems that are financial, marital, job-related, family-related, business-oriented, or anything else that concerns us in life. That is what Jesus is talking about.

'Consider the Lilies of the Field'

Throughout these verses, Jesus is saying again and again, "Why are you worried and fretting about these physical things?" And in verse 28, He specifically says not to worry about our "raiment" — the clothes we will wear. It says:

> **And why take ye thought for raiment? Consider the lilies of the field, how they grow; they toil not, neither do they spin.**
> **— Matthew 6:28**

The word "consider" is the Greek word *katamanthano*, which really means *to give serious attention to* or *to really, really study*. And this verse says that we are to seriously study the lilies of the field. In Greek, the phrase "lilies of the field" refers to a lily growing wild in a field. That means nobody is taking care of it; it just sprung up on its own.

When was the last time you stopped to think about a flower, let alone a wild lily, growing in a field? And notice what Jesus says to observe about the lilies: "…Consider the lilies of the field, how they grow; they toil not, neither do they spin" (Matthew 6:28).

Many people spend a lot of time worrying about their clothes and what to put on their bodies, but Jesus says in this verse to study what the wild lilies do: "…They toil not, neither do they spin" (Matthew 6:28). The word "toil" is the Greek word *kopiao*, which describes *the most intense kind of work*. It would be the equivalent of the flower saying, "Ugh, I've got to really work hard to grow."

But flowers don't do that — they just grow. And verse 28 also says, "…Neither do they spin." The word "spin" means *to spin or to fret with worry*. Flowers don't fret or worry about what they're going to look like. They are beautiful without doing anything. And in Matthew 6:29 and 30, Jesus says:

> **And yet I say unto you, That even Solomon in all his glory was not arrayed like one of these. Wherefore, if God so clothe the grass of the field, which to day is, and to morrow is cast into the oven, shall he not much more clothe you, O ye of little faith?**

This passage should urge us to pause and think about how serious Jesus is about what He is saying. The Greek says shall He not *much, much more* clothe you, meaning we are *much, much more* important to the Lord than the lilies or the grass of the field. And the phrase "little faith" is very interesting too. It is the Greek word *oligopistos*, which means those who have *little faith* or *small trust*. This particular word is only used five times in the New Testament, and it is always used in connection with some form of correction or rebuke.

Jesus is saying here, "You are of much, much more value to me than the lilies and grass of the field but look at their example. If I am faithful to clothe them, just imagine how much more I will do to clothe you, you of little faith."

Don't Let Worry Enter Your Mouth

Then in verse 31, Jesus continues, "Therefore take no thought, saying, What shall we eat? or, What shall we drink? or, Wherewithal shall we be clothed?"

The word "therefore" is translated from the Greek word *oun*, which means *consequently* or *as a result of all this*. The Greek literally means *as a result of all this, take no thought; stop worrying and stop being concerned*. And the word "saying" is the Greek word *legontes*, which means *saying and saying something over and over*. It depicts a person who is running his mouth all the time, saying, "I'm just so worried about this. I'm so worried, I'm worried to death."

When people don't get a grip on worry, it ends up in their mouth. They talk about what's concerning them again and again and begin to produce very negative results. This Greek word *legontes* describes a person so consumed with worry that it's now in his mouth, and he's just *saying and saying* what's troubling him.

In response to this, Jesus says, "Therefore take no thought…." In Greek, this literally means *put an end to worry*. Jesus is telling us to stop worrying and stop saying over and over again, "What are we going to eat, drink, or be clothed with?" Then in verse 32, He tells us: "(For after all these things do the Gentiles seek:) for your heavenly Father knoweth that ye have need of all these things."

The word "Father" used here is the Greek word *Pater*, and it is capitalized, describing the ultimate, greatest Father of all. It means the One who cares and nourishes — and that's exactly who our heavenly Father is. He cares for you, He nourishes you, and this verse says that He "knoweth that ye have need of all these things."

The word "knoweth" or "knows" is the Greek word *oida*, which indicates *knowledge gained by observation*. This means God has His eyes on you; He is watching you, and He knows everything that you have need of. And the word "need" is a Greek word that depicts *a deficit, a need*, or *a necessity*. That means our heavenly Father knows about all your deficits. He knows about your financial deficit, He knows about your emotional deficit, and He knows about your physical needs. He knows about everything you need and all that concerns you.

Seek His Kingdom First

Lastly, Jesus says, "But seek ye first the kingdom of God, and his righteousness; and all these things shall be added unto you" (Matthew 6:33).

The word "but" in Greek is the little preposition *de*, and it means *but instead*. This portion of the verse would actually be better translated as "But instead, on the other hand, or on the contrary seek ye first the kingdom of God." The word "first" is the Greek word *proton*, and it means *first and foremost*. In other words, Jesus is saying, "But instead, first and foremost, make this your primary objective above all else — seek the kingdom of God."

The word "seek" in Greek really means *to seek very enthusiastically*. God does not want us to do this out of obligation. Instead, He is telling us to *enthusiastically* put our energy and focus into seeking His kingdom and His righteousness. And when we do this, He says, "And all these things shall be added unto you."

Jesus is talking about physical things — our deficits, needs, and necessities — all of these things we are lacking shall be added to us. And the word "added" means *to physically add*. These things will be physically added unto you. The phrase "unto you" is the Greek word *humin*, which means *directly to you*.

This passage clearly tells us that our worry cannot add any length to our life — not even 18 inches! It can't add a single thing to our life. But our heavenly Father sees us and knows what we need. So we choose to seek — or to enthusiastically search for — the kingdom of God first, and God will make sure that all the things we need will come our way. This is His promise to us.

If you will get your eyes off of the things you need and seek first and foremost the kingdom of God and His righteousness, our heavenly Father will add to you all the physical things that you need right now. That is the promise of God — and if you'll do this, you will lose all the excess weight of worry, care, concern, and anxiety that you've been carrying in your life.

In the next lesson, we are going to learn from Scripture and Rick's personal experience *how* to stop worrying.

STUDY QUESTIONS

**Study to shew thyself approved unto God, a workman that needeth
not to be ashamed, rightly dividing the word of truth.
— 2 Timothy 2:15**

1.   What was it about Matthew 6:25 that Rick did not like? Why was this a difficult verse for him to apply to his life?

2.   In verse 26, we are told to "behold" the birds of the air, and in verse 28, we are told to "consider" the lilies of the field. What do these two words have in common? What is Jesus asking us to do in each instance?

3.   Why is it so dangerous for worry to get in our mouth? What does this cause someone to do?

4.   Read Matthew 6:32 and 33. What does Jesus tell us to seek instead of our physical needs? Take a moment to really reflect on your answer.

PRACTICAL APPLICATION

**But be ye doers of the word, and not hearers only,
deceiving your own selves.
— James 1:22**

1.   In this lesson, Rick shared about growing up in a home where worry was a common response his parents had when it was time to shop for new school clothes or when bills needed to be paid. Did you have a similar experience? Share about a time when you observed worry in your own life or in the life of a loved one.

2.   In Matthew 6:26-30, Jesus gives us multiple examples of living things that never worry, and yet their needs are met by our heavenly Father. Why do you think He chose birds, lilies, and grass as examples? What can we learn from them?

3.   Verse 32 says that our Father *knows* what we need because He is watching us and has His eyes on us. If God has His eyes on you, what do you think He sees? What is a need in your life that you can entrust to Him today?

TOPIC

How To Stop Worrying

SCRIPTURES

1. **1 Peter 5:7** — Casting all your care upon him; for he careth for you.

2. **1 Peter 5:8** — Be sober, be vigilant; because your adversary the devil, as a roaring lion, walketh about, seeking whom he may devour.

3. **James 4:7** — Submit yourselves therefore to God. Resist the devil, and he will flee from you.

GREEK WORDS

1. "casting" — ἐπιρρίπτω (*epirripto*): to hurl, throw, or cast; to throw or fling something with great force; in secular literature, it often pictured the flinging of a garment, bag, or excess weight off the shoulders of a traveler and onto the back of a beast, such as a donkey, camel, or horse

2. "all" — πᾶσαν (*pasan*): all; all-inclusive; absolutely everything

3. "care" — μέριμνα (*merimna*): anxiety; used to describe affliction, difficulty, hardship, misfortune, trouble, or a complicated circumstance that arises as a result of problems that develop in life: problems that are financial, marital, job-related, family-related, business-oriented, or anything else that concerns us in the earthly realm

4. "upon" — ἐπί (*epi*): on; upon; literally, onto

5. "for" — ὅτι (*hoti*): precisely because

6. "he careth" — μέλει (*melei*): aware, concerned, interested, or thoughtful; one who notices and gives meticulous attention; depicts a thorough and careful focus on the needs of another

7. "for" — περί (*peri*): around; concerning; everything concerning you

8. "sober" — νήφω (*nepho*): to be sober, not drunk; to be free from the deliriums, delusions, and hallucinations that may accompany drunkenness; to think straight, not like a silly drunk; to be free of silly thinking and, hence, able to have presence of mind and clear judgment, enabling one to be in control of his thinking rather than be controlled by urges, impulses, whims, and fluctuating emotions;

to have one's wits about him; to be rational, the opposite of irrational;
to be free from a drunken state in which one drops his guard and is
more likely to give way to foolish behavior, unreasonable conversations, and detrimental decisions; to be serious-minded

9. "vigilant" — **γρηγορέω** (*gregoreo*): to arouse from sleep; to be awake,
   as opposed to being sleepy and negligent; to be watchful, as opposed
   to careless and non-attentive; to give strict attention to; to be cautious;
   to be watchful; to be on high alert; to put up one's guard against a
   sinister outside force or enemy

10. "adversary" — **ἀντίδικος** (*antidikos*): a lawyer who argues in a court
    of law; a prosecuting attorney; a prosecutor who argues vehemently
    against the accused; an accuser who attempts to bring a guilty charge
    against a person on the basis of information from past actions or
    deeds; an attorney who brings formal charges against the accused
    based on some legal violation

11. "devour" — **καταπίνω** (*katapino*): drink down; slurp down; total
    consumption

12. "submit" — **ὑποτάσσω** (*hupotasso*): one who is submitted to some
    type of authority; describes submission to authority in any context;
    to hide behind someone's back, showing that there is protection in
    submission

13. "resist" — **ἀνθίστημι** (*anthistemi*): to stand against; to stand in oppo-
    sition; it demonstrates the attitude of one who is fiercely opposed
    to something and therefore determines to do everything within his
    power to resist it; to stand against it; to withstand; to defy; militarily,
    it was used to depict a preplanned resistance

14. "flee" — **φεύγω** (*pheugo*): to take flight, to run as fast as possible,
    or to escape; it is the picture of one's feet flying as he runs from a
    situation; was used to depict a lawbreaker who fled in terror from a
    city or nation where he broke the law

SYNOPSIS

In Lessons 1 and 2, we learned the importance of casting our care on
the Lord and trusting Him to satisfy our physical needs. We saw that no
matter how strong or determined we think we are, we were never meant
to carry the weight of our own cares and worry. Carrying that burden
alone begins to break us down and affects every part of our life and our

perspective. Instead, we can cast our care on the Lord — He is strong enough to carry it and He knows and cares deeply for the needs in our life.

In this lesson, we are going to see how to put an end to worry. When we don't stop worry from creeping into our life, it begins to drag us down and warps our perspective of things. More than that, it also opens a door to the enemy to find entrance into our life. But that's not the life that Jesus has called us to live! As we examine two new verses, we will see how to finally let go of worry and its damaging effects and learn how to resist the devil and stop him from gaining entrance into our life.

The emphasis of this lesson:

We have a real enemy who is trying to find entrance into our life. Holding onto our worry and care only throws open the door to our life for the devil to come in. The Bible tells us to be sober and vigilant and to let go of worry. When we don't cast our care on the Lord, it weighs us down and opens a door for the devil to attack us.

In the first lesson, Rick shared that as a younger man, he worried about everything. In fact, he was inadvertently trained to worry, so he worried about many things, and this pattern continued throughout his life.

As a teenager, he worried. When he went off to college, he worried. And when he married Denise, he worried. Eventually, Rick ended up in the hospital with bleeding ulcers because he could not put an end to the worry in his life.

Most of Rick's worry was imagined. He worried about things that didn't exist and was concerned about things that might happen but never did. It was like he had become drunk on worry, and those cares were being used by the devil to eat him alive.

But that's not the end of the story. Rick experienced the liberating power of First Peter 5:7, and he has continued to live in that freedom for many, many years. He experienced supernatural weight loss first-hand and now knows what it means to live a worry-free life. And that power is available to every single one of us.

Our anchor verse, First Peter 5:7, tells us, "Casting all your care upon him; for he careth for you."

We have seen in previous lessons that Jesus is pleading with us through this verse to truly cast all of our cares onto Him. Again, the word "casting" is the Greek word *epirripto*, which means *to hurl*, *to throw*, *to cast*, or *to throw or fling something with great force*. It is an action that takes deliberation and intentionality.

In secular literature, "casting" is often portrayed as the flinging of a garment, bag, or excess weight off the shoulders of a traveler and onto the back of a beast, like a donkey, a camel, or a horse.

And that's really what this verse is talking about. It's addressing any person who is carrying so much weight that it's beginning to debilitate him. Maybe the burden is affecting him emotionally, maybe it's affecting his relationships, or maybe it's affecting his perspective of things. It's affecting that person's health, and it's breaking him under a crushing weight.

First Peter 5:7 tells us to cast *all* our care upon Jesus. And the word "all" is an all-encompassing term that means *everything*. It literally means that it is God's will for you to be free of every care and worry. He wants you to be worry-free and care-free, casting all — absolutely all — of your cares on Him.

This verse says that Jesus has come alongside you, and He's saying to you, "You don't have to carry that weight. I'll carry it for you. My shoulders are bigger than yours. Your shoulders were not designed to carry this crushing weight."

Jesus wants you to release anything that's weighing you down. So if you're worried about your spouse or your finances or anything else, heave upward and push over or roll that burden onto Him. Jesus will carry it for you. The burden won't disappear, but His shoulders are big enough to carry it, and you can walk free alongside Him.

This is Jesus' personal invitation to each of us, and it can happen right now. No matter where you are today, you can shed all that weight by simply saying, "Lord, I'm surrendering. I'm going to roll every worry, care, and concern onto you."

Be Sober and Be Vigilant

First Peter 5:7 clearly states that Jesus wants each of us to roll our burdens over onto Him. But in this lesson, we're going to see what happens when we choose *not* to.

First Peter 5:8 says:

Be sober, be vigilant; because your adversary the devil, as a roaring lion, walketh about, seeking whom he may devour.

Notice how the verse begins. It says, "Be sober…." The word "sober" is the Greek word *nepho*, which means *to be sober, not drunk* and *to be free from the deliriums, delusions, and hallucinations that may accompany drunkenness*. It describes someone who thinks straight, not like a silly drunk. It could even be translated "to be free of silly thinking and able to have the presence of mind and clear judgment, enabling one to be in control of his thinking rather than be controlled by urges, impulses, whims, and fluctuating emotions."

In other words, being *sober* means having one's wits about himself, being rational, or being the opposite of irrational. This depicts someone who is free from a drunken state in which one drops his guard and is more likely to give way to foolish behavior, unreasonable conversations, and detrimental decisions. Instead, he is serious-minded and free from the intoxications of life.

In context with verse 7, the word "sober" also pictures someone who is not burdened by all the weight, concerns, anxieties, and worries of life. But when a person chooses to carry all that weight and worry on his own, he becomes drunk with the cares of life.

This person becomes intoxicated with worry; He begins to have delirium and his worry becomes imaginary. Just like someone who is drunk, he starts to see things that don't even exist, but he worries about them nonetheless. And when someone becomes intoxicated with the cares of life, it throws him into a really bad place.

So instead of carrying this weight on our own, the Bible urges us to be sober-minded — to be free from the intoxications of life. And then it says to be *vigilant*. The word "vigilant" is the Greek word *gregoreo*, which is actually where we get the name Greg or Gregory.

This word "vigilant," the Greek word *gregoreo*, means *to arouse from sleep* or *to be awake as opposed to being sleepy and negligent*. It pictures one who is watchful and attentive, and it means *to give strict attention to; to be cautious; to be watchful; to be on high alert*, or *to put up one's guard against a sinister, outside force or enemy*. It could even be translated "to stay wide awake and alert." This particular word for vigilant is only used when there's some kind of sinister force on the outside that's trying to find its way inside.

If you knew that there was some evil force trying to get in to do harm to you or to your family, you would be *vigilant* to do all you could to build a barricade to keep that force on the outside. And that is exactly what First Peter 5:8 is telling us to do.

If you're walking under a burden of care, worry, and anxiety, then you are not successfully fortifying or building a barricade around your life. Instead, you are leaving a door wide open for the devil to find entrance into your life. To close this door, you need to throw all that worry and anxiety onto Jesus so that you are not leaving any entry points open to your adversary the devil.

Know Who Your Adversary Is

The word "adversary" is a very interesting Greek word that is rarely translated correctly. Here it's translated as the word "adversary," but in fact, it is the Greek word *antidikos*, which is the Greek word used to depict *a lawyer who argues in a court of law*. Not only that, but it also particularly means *a prosecuting attorney*.

A prosecutor argues against the accused, bringing a charge of guilt against that person on the basis of something that he's done. Usually, the attorney brings a formal charge against the accused based on some kind of legal violation, or the attorney could be looking for a loophole.

The use of this word in verse 8 tells us that the devil is very, very serious about attacking us and getting on the inside. He'll walk around and around us just looking for some kind of loophole that he can use to get into our life so he can prosecute us and take us down. In fact, First Peter 5:8 could be interpreted like this:

> **Be sober and be vigilant because the devil like a prosecuting attorney is searching for some loophole in your life, some place of spiritual violation where you have broken a spiritual law, and like a prosecuting attorney, he will try to use that evidence to prosecute you and take you down.**

The loophole the devil often uses to enter your life is care and worry. It just throws the door wide open for the devil to come in and affect your marriage, your finances, your health, and your emotions. His constant attacks then begin to deteriorate you and wear you down because you are already carrying something that your shoulders are not strong enough to bear.

Verse 8 goes on to say what the devil will do to you if you don't roll your burden over onto the Lord. It says, "Be sober, be vigilant; because your adversary the devil, as a roaring lion, walketh about, seeking whom he may devour."

The phrase "seeking whom" implies that the devil cannot devour everyone, so he is looking for the one that he *can* devour. And if we read this in context, we see that the one person he can devour is the one who is carrying all those weights and burdens by himself. That is why it is essential for each of us to experience supernatural weight loss. We have to get rid of that weight so we can be free. As long as we are carrying worry and fret, we are in a position for the devil to attack us and take us down.

This verse goes on to say that the devil wants to *devour* us. The word "devour" is the Greek word *katapino*, which is a compound of the words *kata* and *pino*. The word *pino* means *to drink*, but when you compound it together with the word *kata*, it means *to drink down* or *to slurp down*.

This is not describing a lion that is eating the meat of something he has killed — in this picture, the meat is already gone and now there's nothing left but juices. It is describing a lion hovering over the juices of his kill, slurping up what remains. This means that the devil's intention is not just to attack you and victimize you, but he wants to eat you, devour you, and then slurp up everything that remains of you. His goal is total consumption.

Submit To God and Resist the Devil

The devil's goal is to totally consume you, but the good news is you don't have to be that victim. James 4:7 gloriously says:

> **Submit yourselves therefore to God. Resist the devil, and he will flee from you.**

If you are in a position where you are being devoured right now, then do what James 4:7 says to do: Submit yourself to God then resist the devil, and he will flee from you.

But notice before you resist the devil, this verse says you need to *submit* yourselves therefore to God. The word "submit" is the Greek word *hupotasso*, which is a military term and a compound of the words *hupo* and *tasso*. The word *hupo* means *to be under*, and the word *tasso* means *to arrange yourself*, so when these two words are compounded, it pictures one who is submitted or who has arranged himself under some kind of authority.

This word also means *to hide behind someone's back*. When you're submitted to authority, you are not out there on your own. You're hiding behind someone else's back, which means somebody is with you who is protecting you. In this case, it's God — you're hiding behind God's back. This shows us that there is protection in submission. So, again, if you are in a position where you're being devoured, simply begin by saying, "Lord, I'm in a mess. I repent for carrying this weight by myself, and I choose to submit myself to Your authority instead."

Next, James 4:7 says to "*resist* the devil." The word "resist" is the Greek word *anthistemi*, which means *to stand against* or *to stand in opposition*. It demonstrates the attitude of one who is fiercely opposed to something, and therefore, determines to do everything within his power to resist it, to stand against it, to withstand it, or to defy it. That means if we put everything we have into standing against the enemy, this verse promises he will *flee* from us.

The word "flee" is a Greek word that means *to take flight*; *to run as fast as possible*; or *to escape pressure*. It pictures one whose feet are flying as he runs from a situation, and it was used in ancient times to depict a lawbreaker who fled in terror from a city or nation where he had broken the law. This tells us that if we resist the devil with the authority of the Word of God in the name of Jesus and in the power of the Holy Spirit, then, like a lawbreaker, the devil will hit the road.

The devil will run from us when we begin to put pressure on him, but it begins when we choose to repent of worry and submit ourselves to God. Once we have done that, then we will be in a position where we can resist the devil and he'll flee from us.

We have seen in this lesson how to put a stop to worry, and in the next lesson, we will walk through five simple steps that will show us how to move from turmoil into peace.

STUDY QUESTIONS

**Study to shew thyself approved unto God, a workman that needeth
not to be ashamed, rightly dividing the word of truth.
— 2 Timothy 2:15**

1. What does it mean to be "sober," as it is used in First Peter 5:8?
    What does this have to do with the worry and care in your life?

2. Why is it important for you to be vigilant? What does First Peter 5:8
    tell you about the enemy that is trying to find a way into your life?

3. Why does James 4:7 say to "submit" to God? What is the purpose of
    submitting? What does submitting do for you?

4. Read Ephesians 6:10 and 13. What do these verses say about resisting
    the devil? How does this inform your understanding of James 4:7?

PRACTICAL APPLICATION

**But be ye doers of the word, and not hearers only,
deceiving your own selves.
— James 1:22**

1. Has the burden of worry in your life left a door wide open to the
    devil? How can you close that door and ensure it remains shut?

2. The Greek word for "adversary" tells us that the devil is like a prose-
    cuting attorney. Have you experienced the devil accusing you about
    something? What does James 4:7 say the devil will do when you resist
    him?

3. First Peter 5:8 commands us to be sober and not to be intoxicated
    with the cares of this life. What are some actions you can take in your
    daily life to make sure you don't get bogged down with fret or worry
    so you can remain sober minded?

TOPIC

Steps To Move From Anxiety and Worry to a Peace-Filled Life

SCRIPTURES

1. **1 Peter 5:7** — Casting all your care upon him; for he careth for you.

2. **Philippians 4:6** — Be careful for nothing; but in every thing by prayer and supplication with thanksgiving let your requests be made known unto God.

3. **Philippians 4:7** — And the peace of God, which passeth all understanding, shall keep your hearts and minds through Christ Jesus.

GREEK WORDS

1. "casting" — ἐπιρρίπτω (*epirripto*): to hurl, throw, or cast; to throw or fling something with great force; in secular literature, it often pictured the flinging of a garment, bag, or excess weight off the shoulders of a traveler and onto the back of a beast, such as a donkey, camel, or horse

2. "all" — πᾶσαν (*pasan*): all; all-inclusive; absolutely everything

3. "care" — μέριμνα (*merimna*): anxiety; used to describe affliction, difficulty, hardship, misfortune, trouble, or a complicated circumstance that arises as a result of problems that develop in life: problems that are financial, marital, job-related, family-related, business-oriented, or anything else that concerns us in the earthly realm

4. "upon" — ἐπί (*epi*): on; upon; literally, onto

5. "for" — ὅτι (*hoti*): precisely because

6. "he careth" — μέλει (*melei*): aware, concerned, interested, or thoughtful; one who notices and gives meticulous attention; depicts a thorough and careful focus on the needs of another

7. "for" — περί (*peri*): around; concerning; everything concerning you

8. "be careful" — μέριμνα (*merimna*): anxiety; used to describe affliction, difficulty, hardship, misfortune, trouble, or a complicated circumstance that arises as a result of problems that develop in life: problems that

are financial, marital, job-related, family-related, business-oriented, or anything else that concerns us in the earthly realm

9. "nothing" — **μηδέν** (*meden*): absolutely nothing at all

10. "but" — **ἀλλά** (*alla*): but instead

11. "in everything" — **ἐν παντὶ** (*en panti*): in every little thing; in every matter

12. "prayer" — **προσεύχομαι** (*proseuchomai*): compound of **πρός** (*pros*) and **εὔχομαι** (*euchomai*); the word **πρός** (*pros*) means toward and implies closeness; the word **εὔχομαι** (*euchomai*) means to offer a request or to make a vow; idea of an exchange; most commonly used word for prayer in the New Testament

13. "supplication" — **δέησις** (*deesis*): second most often used word for "prayer" in the New Testament; pictures a person with some kind of urgent need or desire in his or her personal life; as time passed, this began to take on the meaning of prayer — the kind of prayer that expresses one's basic needs and wants to God

14. "thanksgiving" — **εὐχαριστέω** (*eucharisteo*): compound of the words (*eu*) and (*charistia*); the word (*eu*) describes something that is good or well and denotes a general good disposition or feeling about something; the word (*charistia*) is from the word (*charis*), the word for grace; compounded, (*eucharistia*) refers to wonderful feelings and good sentiments that freely flow up out of the heart in response to something

15. "requests" — **αἰτέω** (*aiteo*): I ask or I demand

16. "known" — **γνωρίζω** (*gnoridzo*): to make a thing known; to declare something; to broadcast something; to make something very evident

17. "passeth" — **ὑπερέχω** (*huperecho*): a compound of the words **ὑπέρ** (*huper*) and **ἔχω** (*echo*); the preposition **ὑπέρ** (*huper*) means over, above, and beyond; depicts something that is way beyond measure; the idea of superiority; something that is utmost, paramount, foremost, first-rate, first-class, and top-notch; greater, higher, and better than; superior to; preeminent, dominant, and incomparable; more than a match for; unsurpassed or unequaled

SYNOPSIS

In Lesson 1, we saw that Jesus wants to come alongside us and carry the weight of our cares for us. And in Lesson 2, we learned that we don't have to worry about the physical needs in our life because our heavenly Father knows what we need and wants to provide for us.

In Lesson 3, we discovered what happens when we choose to hold on to worry instead of letting it go. We also learned how to stop worrying and, instead, to be sober-minded and vigilant.

As we dive into Lesson 4, we are going to see that by taking five simple steps we can move away from turmoil and anxiety and enter into a peace-filled life. God never intended for you to walk in worry, and these five steps will help you unlock the key to His supernatural peace.

The emphasis of this lesson:

You don't have to care for anything. Instead, God wants you to draw near to Him in prayer so you can surrender your worries and receive His peace. Come boldly to God, make your requests known to Him, and allow His superior, unsurpassed peace to dominate your life.

From First Peter 5:7, we have seen that in order to let go of worry we need to cast our burdens onto the Lord. It says, "Casting all your care upon him; for he careth for you."

The word "casting," as we've seen in previous lessons, is the Greek word *epirripto*, and it means *to hurl*; *to throw*; *to cast*; or *to throw or fling something with great force*. It describes a very intentional action, and it pictures someone who has been carrying around a debilitating amount of weight and finally says, "Hey, I'm not going to carry this anymore," and hurls it off of his shoulders onto an animal, like a camel, horse, or donkey.

Just like those animals, Jesus has come alongside us, and He's saying, "Let me be your beast of burden. Let me carry this heavy weight for you." Just like travelers in the ancient world would push up and roll all that excess weight onto the back of a camel, horse, or donkey, Jesus invites us to roll all that worry and anxiety off of our shoulders and throw it onto Him.

Then First Peter 5:7 says, "Casting *all* your care upon him…."

The word "all" literally means *all* or *absolutely everything*, meaning there's nothing that you cannot roll over onto the shoulders of Jesus. And the word "care," again, is the Greek word *merimna*, which we've seen in several of our lessons. It describes *anxiety*, and it is used to depict affliction, difficulty, or hardships of any kind, such as financial, marital, job-related, or family-related problems.

This verse tells us to cast our cares upon Jesus because He really does care for us. Jesus sees the load you are carrying, and He is coming alongside you saying, "Don't do it. Don't try to carry that on your own. My shoulders are bigger than yours. I really care for you, so let me carry that for you." He cares for everything concerning you, and He wants to carry that weight of worry for you.

'Be Careful for Nothing'

Another verse that exhorts us to let go of worry is Philippians 4:6. On the program, Rick shared that when he was younger this was also a difficult verse for him. He didn't like studying it because this verse begins by saying not to worry — and Rick's life was consumed with worry. Back then he thought worry was a normal part of life, and he definitely didn't know how to stop worrying or how to live a worry-free life.

But as we take a closer look at this verse, we will see that it provides us with five powerful steps that will help us to let go of worry and, instead, choose God's peace. Philippians 4:6 says:

> **Be careful for nothing; but in every thing by prayer and supplication with thanksgiving let your requests be made known unto God.**

The very first words in this verse tell us to "Be careful for nothing…," and the Greek literally means *care for nothing at all*. Again, the word "care" or "careful" is the Greek word *merimna*, and it is used here to describe *anything that makes you anxious*.

This Greek word encompasses anything that we perceive as an affliction, a difficulty, a hardship, or any situation in our life that is filled with misfortune or trouble. All of that is included in this word "care," which appears again and again in Scripture. It pictures any kind of problem that concerns us in the earthly realm. And by showing up again in this verse — it is as though the Holy Spirit is crying out to us through Scripture to really hear what He is saying.

From the very beginning, this verse tells us not to worry about anything or any problem. Immediately, it says, "Cast it over onto the Lord. Don't worry about it for a second." In fact, this phrase in Greek is written as a direct form of speech, which means this is not a suggestion — this is a command telling us not to worry about anything at all.

Then verse 6 tells us what to do instead of worrying. It says, "…But in every thing…." The word "but" in Greek is the word *alla*. Although, a better translation would be "but instead" or "but on the other hand." The words "in everything" are *en panti* in Greek, which mean *in every matter* or *in every little thing* you face. This denotes *everything* — every situation and every moment, big or small.

So instead of worrying or caring about all the things in our life, this verse tells us there is another way to live. In other words, this verse is going to give us five simple steps that will lead us out of a state of turmoil and into a state of peace.

Instead of Worrying — Pray!

The first thing we are told to do is to pray. Philippians 4:6 says, "Be careful for nothing; but in every thing by *prayer*…."

This particular word for prayer is the most commonly used word for prayer in the New Testament. It's a compound of two Greek words. The first part of the word is *pros*, which means *toward* and implies closeness or intimacy. The second part of the word is *euchomai*, and it means *to offer a request* or *to make a vow*.

When you compound these two Greek words, it forms the word *proseuchomai*, which pictures one who draws very, very close to God in prayer. It describes someone who comes into a place where, suddenly, he's face to face with God, and while he's in that position with God, he makes a vow in order to obtain some kind of an exchange.

The best example in Scripture of this word *proseuchomai* — translated as "prayer" — is in the story of Hannah in First Samuel 1. Hannah had been praying for a child for many years, and year after year she went up to Shiloh and lay before the Lord, pouring her heart out. She desperately wanted a child, and finally, Hannah came to a place of *proseuchomai*, where she drew very near to the Lord and made a vow in exchange for that child.

So in this word "prayer," we really find the idea of surrender. When we're tempted to be concerned and consumed with worry, trying to carry it all by ourselves, that is the moment for us to *pros* — get close to the Lord. We need to draw near and say, "Lord, I am here to make a divine exchange. I want to give you my burden and my troubles — all those things that concern me — and in exchange I'm asking you to give me your peace."

This is step number one. We need to draw near to God and give Him our problems in exchange for His peace. That is our divine exchange.

Present Your Petition to God

Philippians 4:6 goes on to say, "…But in every thing by prayer and *supplication*…." The word "supplication" in Greek is the word *deesis*, which describes *a very strong petition*. This tells us that when we draw near to the Lord in prayer, we don't need to be mealy-mouthed. Instead, we can boldly express our petitions to God.

The word "supplication," or *deesis*, really depicts someone who comes forward boldly, earnestly, and strongly, passionately crying out for someone to help or to assist him. It depicts a passionate, earnest, heartfelt, and sincere prayer. Again, this tells us that when we come before the Lord, we don't need to be timid. We can be straightforward and tell God exactly what we feel, exactly what we're facing, and exactly what we would like Him to do.

We've covered the first two steps to move from a place of anxiety and worry to a peace-filled life. Number one: Come to a place of surrender where you make a divine exchange. Number two: Make your petition very clear and present it to God boldly.

Give Thanks Before Your Answer Comes

This brings us to step number three. Philippians 4:6 continues: "…But in every thing by prayer and supplication with *thanksgiving* let your requests be made known unto God."

The word "thanksgiving" is the Greek word *eucharisteo*, and it's a compound of the word *eu* and the word *charistia*. The word *eu* describes *something that is good* or *something that is swell*, and it denotes a generally good disposition or feeling about something. The word *charistia* is from the word *charis*, which is the Greek word for grace.

When you compound these two words, this word "thanksgiving," the Greek word *eucharisteo*, refers to *wonderful feelings and good sentiments that freely flow up out of the heart in response to something* that you've asked God to do, or in response to something God has already done for you.

With the use of this word, the apostle Paul was teaching us that when we earnestly present our petitions to God and ask Him to do something special for us, we need to match it with thanksgiving. We need to offer God an earnest outpouring of our gratitude and praise even though the request may not have been manifested yet.

This is a very important step for us to take in order to move from a state of turmoil, anxiety, and worry into a state of peace. It is not only right to thank God in advance, but it also allows us to demonstrate our faith. And God always rewards faith.

God doesn't just want us to be bold, He also expects us to exercise our faith and thank Him for being good to us even if we're thanking Him in advance. So as we pray, let's throw open our arms and begin to thank Him in advance for what He's going to do.

And when we start filling our mind and mouth with thanksgiving, we'll also start to forget about all the things that we've been worried about because we are choosing, instead, to focus on the goodness of God. This is our third step in moving from fret, turmoil, and worry into a state of peace: Fill your mind and fill your mouth with thanksgiving.

Make Your Faith-Filled Request

Next, Philippians 4:6 tells us, "…Let your requests be known unto God." The word "request" in Greek is the word *aiteo*, and it pictures someone saying, "I ask," or "I demand," and has a full expectation to receive what has been requested. It describes someone asking for something in faith. This is not someone wishfully thinking, *Well, I hope this happens.* This is someone asking — in faith — who says, "God I know you're going to do it."

When we pray, we need to walk away from that place with God fully assured that what we have requested is what we're going to receive. And as long as our prayers, requests, and petitions are based on the Word of God, we can be confident that God is going to move and answer our requests.

That's really what this word "request" means — to request with full expectation. And that gives us step number four: Make your request to God fully expecting Him to answer you.

Make Your Request 'Known'

Finally, we come to step number five. Philippians 4:6 says, "…But in every thing by prayer and supplication with thanksgiving let your requests be made known unto God."

The word "known" is a Greek word that means *to make a thing known* or *to declare something*. It could even be translated "to broadcast something" or "to make something very evident." This tells us that when we pray, we need to declare what we need. We need to broadcast it so loudly that all of Heaven hears our request.

God does not want us to hide what we're asking Him for. He wants us to loudly and boldly make our request known to Him, demonstrating our faith so He can respond to it.

God's Supernatural Peace

In this lesson, we have looked at five simple steps that we can take to walk out of a life of turmoil and into a life filled with peace. Let's review these steps one more time:

Step 1: Come to a place of surrender and divine exchange.

Step 2: Present your petition to God clearly and boldly.

Step 3: Fill your mind and mouth with thanksgiving.

Step 4: Request what you need God to do and believe He will do it.

Step 5: Declare your request so loudly that all of Heaven can hear it.

If you will walk through all five of these steps, you will experience a life filled with the supernatural peace of God. And what is the peace of God like? Philippians 4:7 says:

And the peace of God, which passeth all understanding, shall keep your hearts and minds through Christ Jesus.

The word "passeth" is the Greek word *huperecho*, and it is a compound of the words *huper* and *echo*. The word *huper* is a preposition that means *over, above,* and *beyond*. It depicts something that is way beyond measure and captures the idea of *superiority* or something that is *utmost, paramount, foremost, first-rate, first-class*, and *top-notch*. In other words, it is something that is greater, higher, and better than anything else.

God's peace is superior to, incomparable to, and more than a match for any other kind of peace. It is unsurpassed and unequaled. And that is the kind of peace that God wants to give you — a peace so superior that it is held in a separate category from every other kind of peace. It is a peace that transcends, outdoes, surpasses, excels, rises above, and goes beyond and over the top of any other kind of peace. This peace of God completely outshines every other peace causing it to stand in a category by itself.

And this verse says that this kind of peace will keep our hearts and minds through Christ Jesus. That really is a divine exchange! When we come to God, drawing near to Him with our troubles, burdens, and worries and laying them down before Him, He gives us His superior, incomparable peace that is unlike any other kind of peace. And suddenly, we have moved from turmoil, anxiety, and worry into a state where the amazing peace of God dominates us and rules us.

This is not a fantasy. If you will walk through these five steps in Philippians 4:6, you really can move into a life where you don't worry about anything at all. That is the life and peace that God is extending to you today.

In our next lesson, we will continue to shed the unnecessary weight of worry and learn how to rest in God. It's going to be powerful!

STUDY QUESTIONS

> **Study to shew thyself approved unto God, a workman that needeth not to be ashamed, rightly dividing the word of truth.**
> **— 2 Timothy 2:15**

1. The opening phrase of Philippians 4:6, "Be careful for nothing," is written as a command. Why is this significant? What can we learn from the Greek language here?

2. The Greek word for "prayer" in verse 6 — *proseuchomai* — is the most common word for prayer used in the New Testament. What kind of picture does this type of prayer describe? What is supposed to take place when we are in that one-on-one place with the Lord?

3. Why is it important for us to thank God *before* we receive the answer to our prayer? What does thanking God do for our mind?

4. What does Philippians 4:7 tell us about the peace of God? How does this peace compare to other kinds of peace?

PRACTICAL APPLICATION

**But be ye doers of the word, and not hearers only,
deceiving your own selves.
—James 1:22**

1. When you become overwhelmed with the cares of life, is it your first instinct to pray? Why or why not?

2. Have you ever known that God not only doesn't want us to worry, but He also directly commands us not to? What new insights have you gained about the meaning of "Be careful for nothing" as it appears in Philippians 4:6?

3. In this lesson, we looked at the story of Hannah in First Samuel 1. Have you ever drawn so near to the Lord in prayer, like Hannah, and made a divine exchange?

4. What was your perspective of the peace of God before reading this lesson? How has your understanding changed after studying Philippians 4:6 and 7 so closely?

LESSON 5

TOPIC

How To Let Peace Umpire Your Emotions

SCRIPTURES

1. **1 Peter 5:7** — Casting all your care upon him; for he careth for you.

2. **2 Thessalonians 1:7** — And to you who are troubled rest with us….

3. **Colossians 3:15** — And let the peace of God rule in your hearts….

GREEK WORDS

1. "casting" — ἐπιρρίπτω (*epirripto*): to hurl, throw, or cast; to throw or fling something with great force; in secular literature, it often pictured the flinging of a garment, bag, or excess weight off the shoulders of a traveler and onto the back of a beast, such as a donkey, camel, or horse

2. "all" — πᾶσαν (*pasan*): all; all-inclusive; absolutely everything

3. "care" — μέριμνα (*merimna*): anxiety; used to describe affliction, difficulty, hardship, misfortune, trouble, or a complicated circumstance that arises as a result of problems that develop in life: problems that are financial, marital, job-related, family-related, business-oriented, or anything else that concerns us in the earthly realm

4. "upon" — ἐπί (*epi*): on; upon; literally, onto

5. "for" — ὅτι (*hoti*): precisely because

6. "he careth" — μέλει (*melei*): aware, concerned, interested, or thoughtful; one who notices and gives meticulous attention; depicts a thorough and careful focus on the needs of another

7. "for" — περί (*peri*): around; concerning; everything concerning you

8. "troubled" — θλῖψις (*thlipsis*): great pressure; crushing pressure; to suffocate; a horribly tight, life-threatening squeeze; a situation so difficult it causes one to feel stressed, squeezed, pressured, or even crushed

9. "rest" — ἄνεσις (*anesis*): to let up; to relax; to stop being stressed; to find relief; used in the secular world to denote the release of a bowstring that has been under great pressure; used figuratively to mean relaxation from the stresses of life and freedom to have a little recreation; relief from the constant stress a person or group of individuals has undergone; to let something go; to shake it off; to relax

10. "peace" — εἰρήνη (*eirene*): pictures the cessation of war; conflict put away; a time of rebuilding and reconstruction after war has ceased; distractions removed; a time of prosperity; the rule of order in the place of chaos; a calm, inner stability that results in the ability to conduct oneself peacefully, even in the midst of circumstances that would normally be traumatic or upsetting; the Greek equivalent for the Hebrew word "shalom," which expresses the idea of wholeness, completeness, or tranquility in the soul that is unaffected by outward circumstances or pressures

11. "rule" — **βραβεύω** (*brabeuo*): used in ancient times to describe the umpire or referee who moderated and judged the athletic competitions that were so popular in the ancient world; hence, to arbitrate, umpire, or referee; an umpire who calls all the shots and makes all the decisions

12. "in your hearts" — **ἐν ταῖς καρδίαις ὑμῶν** (*en tais kardiais humon*): inside your hearts; the word **καρδία** (*kardia*) denoted the human heart and the seat of all emotions; whatever dominated the heart would then affect the whole person

SYNOPSIS

In each lesson, we have been studying how to let go of worry and receive the peace of God instead. In Lesson 1, we saw how Jesus comes alongside us and asks us to throw our worry and care onto His back. In Lesson 2, we learned what the Bible says about our physical needs. God really does not want us to care for anything. Instead, He is asking us to trust Him to meet our needs.

In Lesson 3, we saw the negative consequences of holding on to worry. We also learned what it means to stop worrying and resist the trap of the enemy. In Lesson 4, we examined Philippians 4:6 and 7 and discovered five steps that we can take to move out of turmoil and into a peace-filled life.

In Lesson 5, we will dive even deeper into this topic of peace. We will see that God not only wants us to rest from the troubles of this life, but He also wants us to let His supernatural peace rule in our hearts and dominate our lives. As we take a look at Scripture and Rick's personal testimony, we will see how to shed the burden of worry once and for all and experience the supernatural weight loss God has for us.

The emphasis of this lesson:

Stop wrestling with life and start resting in Jesus. The Bible tells us again and again that we are not supposed to worry about anything. And when we are troubled by life, God tells us to rest. You don't have to relapse into worry like Rick did. You can choose to rest and to stay in peace, letting the peace of God be the umpire that rules your heart, your emotions, and your life. That is God's promise to you.

A Peace-Filled Life

In the last four lessons, we've seen how serious Jesus is when He tells us not to worry. God never intended for us to carry the burden of concern and anxiety in our life. Instead, He has come alongside us, and He's asking us to throw that weight over onto Him. He wants to carry it for us because He *is* strong enough. His shoulders can handle the weight of our worry, and in its place, He wants to give us His supernatural peace.

First Peter 5:7, says: "Casting all your care upon him; for he careth for you."

This verse tells us that Jesus has come alongside us like a beast of burden, and He is ready for us to throw off the weight we've been carrying and cast it onto Him. And He doesn't just want *some* of our care, He wants *all* of it. He wants to bear *everything* — every worry, care, and concern. He wants to carry every situation that is troubling us or complicating our life. This is truly what this verse is saying.

We can trust Jesus with it all because He cares for us. Jesus is not uninterested in our lives; He is meticulously and attentively observing every detail of our lives. He sees when we are carrying a weight that is too heavy for us, and He wants to step in and free us to live a worry-free life.

That is God's will for you according to First Peter 5:7, and this really can become your reality. God wouldn't have said it if it wasn't true. *Right now*, you can move into a peace-filled life and heave all that worry onto Jesus. And in this lesson, we're also going learn how to let peace umpire our emotions.

Take a Break From Worry

In Second Thessalonians, the apostle Paul wrote to the Thessalonian church who was experiencing an intense period of persecution. These early believers were under great stress and such strong opposition that it seemed like all of society was against them. The pressure was unrelenting, and Paul wrote to them, saying:

> **And to you who are troubled rest with us….**
>
> —2 Thessalonians 1:7

The word "troubled" is the Greek word *thlipsis*, which describes *great pressure, crushing pressure*, or pressure so great it could suffocate someone. It depicts *a horribly tight, life-threatening squeeze* or *a situation so difficult that it causes one to feel stressed, squeezed, pressured, or even crushed.* This was the debilitating pressure that the Thessalonian believers were under, and it was nonstop.

Paul wrote to them and said, "Those of you who are under stress, or who are under pressure, *rest with us.*" And the word "rest" is the Greek word *anesis.* It means *to let up; to relax; to stop being stressed;* or *to find relief.*

It was used in the secular world to denote the release of a bowstring that had been under great pressure. And figuratively, it also referred to relaxation from the stresses of life and the freedom to have a little recreation. It pictures relief from the constant stresses that a person or a group of people have undergone for a prolonged season. It was like saying, "Let up, let go, and just shake it off and relax."

Second Thessalonians 1:7 could even be interpreted: "To you who are still going through difficulties right now, it's time for you to let up, take a breather, and relax."

We all know what it's like to be under pressure, but none of us can stay under that kind of stress continuously. As we continue in this lesson, we're going to see how to loosen up a bit, shake off our troubles, and allow ourselves a little relaxation and time for recreation.

Rick's Brief Relapse

Rick mentioned in an earlier lesson that after Jesus delivered him, he did have one relapse where worry re-entered his life. It was very brief, but it was still a very serious situation in his life. Below is Rick's testimony of how the Lord, again, set him free from the devastating weight of worry:

> I really had been worry-free for many years, but then we began a big building project in the Republic of Latvia, which was the newly emerging nation of Latvia from the former Soviet Union. Our family was living there at that time, and we had lived there for nearly ten years.
>
> The Lord led us to construct the first major church building in that region in 55 years. Now, when we began that project, we did not realize how hell was going to try to stand against us, but just try to imagine it. We were in a former communist country where most people still did not believe in God. The government was

against us, and somehow we were going to construct this massive, massive building. Crazy right?

But we did it. The grace of God was empowering us, and by faith, we were pushing and pushing through. Finally, we dug the hole for the building. We had the biggest hole in the nation…but then we ran out of money.

The devil would say to me every day, "What kind of testimony is this? You own the biggest hole in the nation, and you don't even have the money to fill it with sand and gravel and rebar. People are going to laugh at you." And every day the devil was speaking to me and speaking to me, trying to put me under stress. He began to penetrate my mind and my emotions, and I began to worry.

Well, snow came and filled the hole, and I was so grateful for that snow because it gave me an excuse to say we were going to put off building until warmer weather came. Eventually, warmer weather did come, and more money had also come in so we continued building. But the financial needs to build that building just seemed to be unending.

They weren't small sums of money that we needed either. The builder would call and say, "I need $100,000 by next week." Well, we were building with cash, which means we didn't take a loan. And in our part of the world, a church couldn't even get a loan, so we *had* to build it with cash.

The builder called again, saying, "Thanks for the $100,000, but by next week I'll need another $50,000." And then he'd call the next week and say, "I'm going to need $250,000." I mean, the project was just enormous, and we couldn't be late because the government had only given us 22 months to finish the project.

I found myself lapsing into stress and worry. I would just lie in bed at night, thinking, *Oh, dear Jesus, where are we going to get money?* Then the Lord would say to me, "Look how faithful I've been to you. Didn't I just provide what you needed?" And I would say, "Yes, Lord, you did. But how many times can that happen?"

Distress was just controlling me. And when you're drunk on worry, you don't think right, and you don't see right. All I could see was that a mountain of need was in front of us. I couldn't even remember how faithful God had been because all I could see was what was in front of me.

And the stress just kept getting deeper and deeper. Every night I was rolling this way and that way, anticipating another call needing more money and not knowing where we were going to find it. Our partners were faithfully giving, but we just needed more, and it seemed to be nonstop.

Then one night in the middle of the night, I was so disturbed that I couldn't sleep, so I got up out of bed and walked down the long hallway in our apartment to my study. I went into my study, sat in my chair, and laid my head on my desk. Then I began to pray. I was so swamped with worry and anxiety that I found myself at two o'clock in the morning just weeping and weeping, crying out to the Lord.

I said to God, "What are we going to do? Lord, I know you've been faithful, but Lord, how many times can these financial miracles take place? Lord, we need another one, and another one, and another one." And I knew that it was the Lord who asked us to build that building — and He's always faithful — but at that moment, stress, anxiety, and worry were just affecting my perspective. As I laid my head on that desk and just wept and wept, all of a sudden in the middle of my weeping, I felt a little tap on my shoulder.

I remember thinking, *It's the middle of the night. Who would be tapping me on the shoulder? Maybe it's the Lord.* So I pulled my head up from the desk, and there standing next to me was our youngest son Joel. At that time, Joel must have been eight or nine years old.

I said, "Joel what are you doing up in the middle of the night?" I was still crying, and my face was covered with tears. Then Joel said, "Dad, something woke me up and told me to come down here."

He said, "Daddy, why are you crying?" And I said, "Oh, Joel. Daddy is just worried about where we're going to get the finances to build this building." And Joel looked at me, put his hands on his hips, and said, "Ah, Dad, hasn't God proven Himself faithful to you yet?"

Well, you know, it really was the Lord standing by me, speaking to me through Joel. And after Joel spoke those words to me, he turned around and went back down the hallway and went back to bed. And I sat there with these words just ringing in my mind: *Hasn't God proven Himself faithful to you yet?*

I felt like a drunk who had been given a good cup of coffee to sober him up, and suddenly, I said, "Yes, God has been faithful." And in that moment when I began to reflect on the goodness of God, all that fear, all that anxiety, and all that worry just began to melt right off of me.

Right then, I made a decision that I was not going to relapse into worry again. My friend, it really is a decision. And I came to understand the value of Colossians 3:15, which says, "And let the peace of God rule in your hearts, to the which also ye are called in one body; and be ye thankful."

Rick's testimony is a *powerful* example of what the Lord wants to do in your life too. No matter how big the burden you're carrying seems, Jesus has come alongside you and He's saying, "Have I not proven Myself faithful to you yet?" You don't have to carry that weight for one more minute. You can release it into the arms of Jesus, just like Rick did.

Let the Peace of God Rule Your Heart

Colossians 3:15 tells us, "And let the peace of God rule in your hearts, to the which also ye are called in one body; and be ye thankful."

Notice it says "let." Right away we see that we have a part to play — we have to give way to the peace of God and allow it to operate in our life. And then we see the word "peace," which we've been talking about throughout each of these lessons.

So what does the word "peace" mean? It is the Greek word *eirene*, and it describes *the cessation of war* or *when conflict is put away*. It pictures a time of rebuilding and reconstruction that takes place after war has ceased, and it denotes *the removal of distractions, a time of prosperity,* and *the rule of order in the place of chaos.* "Peace" also means *a calm inner stability* that results in the ability to conduct oneself peacefully, even in the midst of circumstances that would normally be traumatic or upsetting.

The word *eirene* is the Greek equivalent of the Hebrew word "shalom," which expresses the idea of *wholeness, completeness,* or *tranquility in the soul* that is unaffected by outward circumstances or pressures. That's what peace is.

Colossians 3:15 continues, "And let the peace of God *rule* in your hearts…." The word "rule" is the wonderful Greek word *brabeuo,* which was used in ancient times to depict *an umpire or referee who moderated and judged the athletic competitions that were so popular in the ancient world.* It also means *to arbitrate, umpire,* or *referee* and describes an umpire who calls all the shots and makes all the decisions. This tells us that the peace of God has been placed in our lives as an umpire to moderate and make decisions. And Colossians 3:15 says that peace is to rule in our *hearts.*

The word "heart" in Greek is the word *kardia.* In the ancient Greek world, the heart was viewed as the seat of all human emotions, so that tells us peace is meant to rule and umpire all our emotions. We also know that our heart pumps blood to the rest of our being, so whatever is going on in our heart really does affect our whole being. For example, if your heart is filled with turmoil, you're going to have turmoil throughout your whole being. But if peace is ruling in your heart, peace is going to affect your whole being and all of your life.

So if you do what this verse says and give way to let the peace of God rule in your life or act as an umpire in your life, God's peace will dominate you and move you into a period of tranquility even if your outward circumstances are traumatic or upsetting. You won't be moved by the outward circumstance anymore because God's peace will be calling the shots in your heart.

Knowing this, Colossians 3:15 could be translated: "Let the peace of God call the shots in your life," or "Let the peace of God be the umpire in your life and over your emotions," or even "And let the peace of God act as a referee in your life and over your emotions."

Let the Peace of God Dominate Your Life

Peace is already in you; you simply need to let it do its job. If you let it, peace will dominate you and fill your heart. It will keep your emotions from pumping chaos, fear, and anxiety throughout your whole system. From your heart, God's peace will dominate you, it will referee your emotions, and it will call the shots in your life. It will keep you in a tranquil place so that you don't relapse into an episode of worry or anxiety.

God really wants every one of us to experience supernatural weight loss and throw off all the worry and weight we've been carrying. He wants us to transition from a life weighed down by worry and concern to a carefree life dominated by peace. Isn't that the best news? And this really can be your reality.

STUDY QUESTIONS

**Study to shew thyself approved unto God, a workman that needeth
not to be ashamed, rightly dividing the word of truth.
— 2 Timothy 2:15**

1. What kind of pressure were the Thessalonian believers facing when Paul wrote to them? What did he tell them to do?
2. In Rick's testimony, he said that the devil was accusing him and trying to discourage him. What Greek word did you learn about in Lesson 3 that describes this kind of accusing behavior?
3. What is the significance of the word "let" in Colossians 3:15? Why is this important in understanding how peace operates in your life?
4. Read John 14:27. How does the definition of God's peace in this lesson inform your understanding of this verse? What does it tell you about how God wants you to live in these last days?

PRACTICAL APPLICATION

**But be ye doers of the word, and not hearers only,
deceiving your own selves.
—James 1:22**

5. Is rest a regular practice in your life? If yes, what does rest look like for you? If no, what are some rhythms of rest that you can begin to incorporate?

6. What led to Rick's relapse into worry? Do you think there was anything he could have done to prevent it?

7. Has worry entered or re-entered your life? Think about the words the Lord spoke to Rick: "Have I not proven Myself faithful to you yet?" Take a moment to ask the Holy Spirit to remind you of the times in your life where He has been faithful to you, then journal those significant moments so you can read and remember them continually.

8. Colossians 3:15 says that God's peace is meant to act like an umpire in your heart. What role has peace had in your life? Are there any changes you need to make in order to allow God's peace to dominate your life?

CLAIM YOUR FREE RESOURCE!

As a way of introducing you further to the teaching ministry of Rick Renner, we would like to send you FREE of charge his teaching, "How To Receive a Miraculous Touch From God" on CD or USB format.

In His earthly ministry, Jesus commonly healed *all* who were sick of *all* their diseases. In this profound message, learn about the manifold dimensions of Christ's wisdom, goodness, power, and love toward all humanity who came to Him in faith with their needs.

☑ **YES, I want to receive Rick Renner's monthly teaching letter!**

Simply scan the QR code to claim this resource or go to: **renner.org/claim-your-free-offer**

R renner.org

f facebook.com/rickrenner • facebook.com/rennerdenise

▶ youtube.com/rennerministries • youtube.com/deniserenner

⃝ instagram.com/rickrenner • instagram.com/rennerministries_
instagram.com/rennerdenise